Irish Chain
in a Day

— Single and Double

By Eleanor Burns

To Orion – A Star!

Illustrations by Patricia Knoechel
Photography by Brian Steutel
Typesetting by Headline
Layout by Letty Butler Brewster

First Printing – June, 1986

Quilt in a Day T.M.
1955 Diamond Street, Unit A
San Marcos, Ca. 92069
(619) 436-8936

Table of Contents

Introduction

I will never forget the magic of Christmas 1955 when my mother gave me my **first** sewing machine. I had to clamp it to the table, hand crank it, and constantly pick out the bobbin threads, but nonetheless, it was wonderful! I wish every mother and child shared the joy of sewing as we did! I wrote the Single Irish Chain Quilt for children and beginners of all ages, and the beautiful Double Irish Chain Quilt for those that **already love** sewing!

My son, Orion, was fascinated as he watched the whirl of my quiltmaking in his toddler years. His older brother Grant and I weren't surprised when he made his first quilt at five "standing and dancing" at the sewing machine. I remember the thrill in his eyes when he made a Christmas stocking for his teacher. He ran to the kitchen to tell me how **happy** he was when he was sewing.

The time I spent with Orion, now ten, sewing the Single Irish Chain was priceless. He used the rotary cutter and sewing machine like a pro, and all the while, shared his helpful hints. He preferred to pin the 45" strips together. It was my job to pin the 3 3/4" strips together so all the points matched. He said, "Look at it this way, Mom, we're doing two things. I'm learning how to sew better, and **you** are learning how to pin better." I approached the ironing board with caution, figuring he would balk at the job. After I demonstrated the "proper" way to iron, Orion said, "I have a great idea! Let's do it this way." He promptly laid the iron down flat and pulled the fabric quickly along under it!

When I presented a deep burgundy colored fabric for the border, creative Orion wasn't pleased with the dull color! Laying near our sewing was a bright red tablecloth waiting to be ironed. You guessed it - its in the quilt!

As Orion finished the last bit of tying, he wiped his brow and said, "Wow, you really got to love somebody when you make them a quilt!" Why don't you make somebody you love a quilt!

Eleanor and Orion Burns

Color Selection

Color Selection

This particular quilt is most appropriate to brighten a room because of the large light area in Block 2. Colors are easy to select with the quilt needing only one light, one medium, and one dark. Traditionally, the light was solid white, or off white, but todays quilters have successfully used a calico with a white or off white backround that looks like a solid from a distance, or any light solid.

The dark creates the "chains" throughout the quilt, and is the dominant color. In the Double Irish Chain, the medium runs in the middle of the two "chains", and can be either a softer tone of the dark, or a contrast color extracted from the dark color.

When selecting your colors, stack and rewrap the fabric bolts so that you see just a small portion of light, dark, medium, dark, and light again. Stand back and squint at the stack to see if you are pleased with the values.

Remember to mix the scales of prints also as a solid, or one that looks like a solid, a small scale print, and a large scale print. A quilt of all the same scale prints tends to look "boring!" Striped fabrics are not appropriate for use in the Irish Chain.

Color Variations

For a completely different but striking look in the Irish Chain, reverse the light and dark colors throughout.

Many traditional Irish Chains were often made with only a concord blue and muslin, or turkey red and muslin. For a two colored Double Irish Chain quilt, add the medium yardage to the light yardage and substitute the light for the medium color in the sewing instructions. Follow this Block 1 (Double) closely when using only two colors:

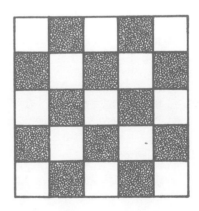

Two Color Double Irish Chain

A   B   C   B   A

Materials and Supplies

Fabric: Select a good quality of 100% cotton 45" wide for your blocks and backing. If you wish, prewash the fabrics separately with soap in a gentle wash cycle. If you do not prewash your fabric before making your quilt, carefully hand wash it the first time in cold water with a delicate soap.

If you choose to use a solid white or off white for your light, avoid inexpensive lining fabrics and muslin with a low thread count that will not stand up with wear and washing.

Batting: Select bonded polyester batting for the inside of your quilt in your choice of thicknesses. The thickest battings, 8 oz. - 10 oz., show the most dimension when tied and are the warmest. A thin batting, 2 - 3 oz., is best for hand quilting. Check for a brand of bonded batting that announces it has not been treated with formaldehyde and has no "needle drag." It should feel soft to the touch, and not fall apart when tugged on. If you are going to "stitch in the ditch" through the borders, practice on various pieces of batting sandwiched between two pieces of fabric to find the best thickness that your machine will stitch through.

Floss: Use all strands of embroidery floss, crochet thread, pearl cotton, candlewicking yarn, or 100% wool yarn for tying down the blocks. To test the durability of a fiber, hold several strands between your fingers and rub the ends briskly. Don't use yarns or fibers that fray easily.

Supplies

Rotary Cutter: Use a large industrial size cutter that is capable of cutting through several layers of fabric at once. **Always keep it closed when not in use.**

Ruler: Use a thick 6" x 12" or 6" x 24" see-thru gridded ruler for accurate measuring. A wooden ruler can not be used with a rotary cutter as the sharp blade digs into the ruler.

Gridded Cutting Mat: This mat of a special plastic material must be used with the rotary cutter and ruler to protect other surfaces and give lasting life to the rotary cutter blade.

Magnetic Seam Guide: This useful tool is excellent when stitching straight, accurate seams in the Irish Chain.

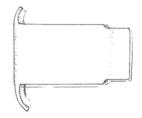

Presser Foot   Magnetic Seam Guide

Presser Foot: Use a general purpose presser foot as illustrated. Use the edge of the foot as a guide for a 1/4" seam allowance. Do not use a foot that results in a skimpy seam allowance.

Thread: Purchase two large spools of polyester spun thread the same shade as your light color.

Pins: Use 1 3/4" extra-long, sharp pins with the colored heads for pinning and a curved upholstery needle for tying.

Overlock Sewing Machine (Optional): Sewing the strips together on an overlock is exceptionally fast, however not necessary.

Quilt Size

Both the Single and Double Irish Chain quilts are coverlets in all bed sizes and need a dust ruffle. The blocks lay on the top of the mattress and the borders cover the sides of the first mattress. If you want a bedspread that drops to the floor, consider making the next size quilt.

Yardage Selection

The yardage charts for both the Single Irish Chain Quilt recommended for beginners and the Double Irish Chain Quilt recommended for advanced sewers follow on pages 8 through 13. Purchase the yardage for either of the quilts in your selected size plus the yardage for one of the borders: either an easy border or seminole border.

Yardage Charts

Baby Quilt

8 Block 1 - 8 Block 2

	Single Chain	OR	Double Chain	AND	Easy Border	OR	Seminole Border
light	1 1/8 yds.		1 yd.				1 yd.
medium	--		1/2 yd.		1/2 yd.		1 1/8 yds.
dark	2/3 yds.		2/3 yds.				3/4 yds.
Bonded Batting:					1 1/4 yds.		3 1/2 yds. or 56" x 56"
Backing:					1 1/4 yds.		3 1/2 yds. or 56" x 56"
Approximate Finished Size:					44" x 44"		53" x 53"

Cutting Chart

	Single Chain		Double Chain		Easy Border		Seminole Border
light	(4) 3 3/4"		(2) 2 1/2"				(8) 2 1/2"
medium	--		(5) 2 1/2"		(4) 3 1/2"		(10) 3 1/2"
dark	(5) 3 3/4"		(8) 2 1/2"				(2) 3 1/2" (4) 2 1/2"

Lap Robe

15 Block 1 - 15 Block 2

	Single Chain	OR	Double Chain	AND	Easy Border	OR	Seminole Border
light	2 yds		1 1/2 yds.				1 1/8 yds.
medium	--		3/4 yd.		1 3/4 yds.		1 3/4 yds.
dark	1 yd.		1 1/4 yds.		1 1/8 yds.		1 yd.

Bonded Batting: 4 1/4 yds. or 71" x 81"

Backing: 4 1/4 yds.

Approximate Finished Size: 68" x 78"

Cutting Chart

	Single Chain		Double Chain		Easy Border		Seminole Border
light	(6) 3 3/4"		(4) 2 1/2"				(10) 3 1/2"
medium	--		(9) 2 1/2"		(12) 4 1/2"		(12) 4 1/2"
dark	(8) 3 3/4"		(16) 2 1/2"		(8) 4 1/2"		(3) 4 1/2" (5) 3 1/2"

Twin Quilt

20 Block 1 - 20 Block 2

	Single Chain	OR	Double Chain	AND	Easy Border	OR	Seminole Border
light	2 1/2 yds.		2 yds.				1 1/4 yds.
medium	--		1 yd.		2 yds.		2 yds.
dark	1 1/4 yds.		1 1/2 yds.		1 1/4 yds.		1 1/8 yds.

Bonded Batting: 6 yds. or 71" x 100"

Backing: 6 yds.

Approximate Finished Size: 68" x 96"

Cutting Chart

	Single Chain		Double Chain		Easy Border		Seminole Border
light	(8) 3 3/4"		(5) 2 1/2"				(12) 3 1/2"
medium	--		(12) 2 1/2"		(14) 4 1/2"		(14) 4 1/2"
dark	(10) 3 3/4"		(20) 2 1/2"		(9) 4 1/2"		(3) 4 1/2" (6) 3 1/2"

Double Quilt

24 Block 1 - 24 Block 2

	Single Chain	OR	Double Chain	AND	Easy Border	OR	Seminole Border
light	3 yds.		2 1/4 yds.				1 1/2 yds.
medium	--		1 1/8 yds.		2 1/8 yds.		2 1/8 yds.
dark	1 1/2 yds.		1 7/8 yds.		1 3/8 yds.		1 1/4 yds.

Bonded Batting: 6 yds. or 81" x 100"

Backing: 6 yds.

Approximate Finished Size: 77" x 96"

Cutting Charts

	Single Chain		Double Chain		Easy Border		Seminole Border
light	(10) 3 3/4"		(6) 2 1/2"				(12) 3 1/2"
medium	--		(14) 2 1/2"		(16) 4 1/2"		(16) 4 1/2"
dark	(13) 3 3/4"		(24) 2 1/2"		(10) 4 1/2"		(3) 4 1/2" (6) 3 1/2"

Queen Quilt
28 Block 1 – 28 Block 2

	Single Chain	OR	Double Chain	AND	Easy Border	OR	Seminole Border
light	3 1/3 yds.		2 2/3 yds.				1 1/2 yds.
medium	--		1 1/4 yds.		2 1/8 yds.		2 1/8 yds.
dark	1 2/3 yds.		2 1/8 yds.		1 3/8 yds.		1 1/4 yds.

Bonded Batting: 6 yds. or 90" x 100"

Backing: 9 yds. or 91" x 101"

Approximate Finished Size: 86" x 96"

Cutting Chart

	Single Chain		Double Chain		Easy Border		Seminole Border
light	(12) 3 3/4"		(8) 2 1/2"				(12) 3 1/2"
medium	--		(16) 2 1/2"		(16) 4 1/2"		(16) 4 1/2"
dark	(15) 3 3/4"		(29) 2 1/2"		(10) 4 1/2"		(3) 4 1/2" (6) 3 1/2"

King Quilt

32 Block 1 – 32 Block 2

	Single Chain	OR	Double Chain	AND	Easy Border	OR	Seminole Border
light	3 2/3 yds.		3 yds.				1 5/8 yds.
medium	--		1 1/2 yds.		2 1/2 yds.		2 1/2 yds.
dark	1 2/3 yds.		2 1/2 yds.		1 1/2 yds.		1 1/4 yds.

Bonded Batting: 6 yds. or 100" x 100"

Backing: 9 yds.

Approximate Finished Size: 96" x 96"

Cutting Chart

	Single Chain		Double Chain		Easy Border		Seminole Border
light	(12) 3 3/4"		(8) 2 1/2"				(14) 3 1/2"
medium	--		(18) 2 1/2"		(18) 4 1/2"		(18) 4 1/2"
dark	(15) 3 3/4"		(32) 2 1/2"		(11) 4 1/2"		(3) 4 1/2" (7) 3 1/2"

Cutting Instructions

The quickest, most accurate method of cutting strips is with a large rotary cutter, a thick gridded, see-thru 6" x 12" or 6" x 24" ruler, and a cutting board.

Tear your fabric to put it on the straight of the grain. Fold the fabric in fourths, matching up the torn straight edge. It is sometimes impossible to match up the selvage sides!

Lay your fabric on the board with most of it laying off to the right. Place the see-thru ruler on the very edge of the fabric on the left.

With your left hand, firmly hold the ruler with 4 fingers. Keep the little finger on the mat to hold the ruler steady.

With the rotary cutter in your right hand, begin cutting with the blade off the fabric on the mat. Put all of your strength into the rotary cutter as you cut away from you and trim off the torn ragged edge.

Move your ruler over every 3 3/4" for the Single Chain, and 2 1/2" for the Double Chain, measuring and cutting carefully and accurately. Follow the charts on pages 8 through 13 for specific information on each quilt. All light strips are not cut at this time. They are cut once Block 1 is made.

Check every few strips to make certain that they are straight. If you are getting crooked strips, tear to put the fabric back on the straight of the grain, refold, and resume your cutting.

If you are left-handed, reverse the cutting process with the fabric on the left and the ruler on the right.

Fabric on right
Ruler on left

Sewing Terms

Assembly Line Sewing, Butting On, and Flashfeeding: All three phrases basically mean the same thing, and are all time savers. Once the first two strips or sections are sewn together, do not raise the presser foot or remove from the machine. Butt on and continuously stitch the second set immediately behind the first. Butt and stitch all pairs together in the same manner.

1/4" Seam Allowance: Check to see if using the edge of your presser foot as a guide gives you a 1/4" seam allowance. A generous 1/4" is preferred to a skimpy one. If using your presser foot as a guide produces a skimpy seam, consider using a magnetic seam guide.

Some machines have the needle off-center to the left, and consequently a wide seam is produced when the edge of the presser foot is used as a guide. Experiment to find the proper adjustment to get that 1/4" seam.

15 Stitches Per Inch: If your sewing machine does not list stitches per inch, but lists numbers from 1 to 4, set the stitch length at 2. It is not necessary to backstitch at the beginning and end of each strip.

Hints for Kids

Cutting Strips: Draw a line at 3 3/4" on the under side of the ruler with a dark marker. Use this line for cutting 45" strips and 3 3/4" sections. When the Single Irish Chain is finished, this line can be scrubbed off.

Pinning Strips: Lay the strips flat and pin before sewing. Pin the sections of Block 1 together also.

Right Sides Together: Since this term is difficult to perceive, say "Put pretty sides together."

Fast Sewing Machines: Fortunately, some machines come with the choice of a fast or slow gear. However, improvisions can be made! If you have a button to push on a foot pedal, suggest the child "tap to the imaginary music" to slow the machine down. If you have a hinge type foot pedal, insert a sponge between the hinge to slow it down. Keep the foot pedal from sliding away from the child's feet by putting it on top of a car's rubber floormat.

Even 1/4" seam allowances: Use the magnetic seam guide so the seam can never get wider than 1/4".

Short Sewing Periods: To avoid careless sewing, be aware of their attention span and quit as soon as they are restless. Keep the sewing sessions close together so there is continuity in learning.

Supervision: Teach them safety rules and watch them closely, especially while they are using the rotary cutter and iron.

Success: Use praise often and make the sewing sessions fun! Avoid criticism! Don't expect perfection and insist on ripping out all imperfect work. Getting a child to love sewing, a possible lifetime hobby, is more important than a perfect quilt.

Single Irish Chain

Making the Sections for Block 1 and Block 2 (Single)

Completed Block 1: It is made up of Sections A and B.

A is used twice.
B is used once.

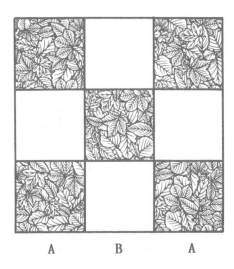

Completed Block 2: It is made of a light square the same size as a completed Block 1.

Section A (Single)

Arrange your strips in this color order.

Stack up this many strips of each color for your particular size quilt.

Baby	2
Lap	3
Twin	4
Double	5
Queen	6
King	6

Place the light strip right sides together to the first dark strip.

Stitch the length of the strip with a 1/4" seam allowance and 15 stitches per inch.

Be accurate with your seam allowance.

Use a magnetic seam guide if you have difficulty keeping a straight, accurate seam.

Butt on and sew the next light and dark strips until they are all stitched.

Open up the dark/light strips.

Add the second dark strip to the dark/light strip.

Butt on and sew the dark strips to all dark/light strips.

Section A looks like this:

Carefully steam press down the
middle of the light strip, pressing
the seams to the dark sides. Press
on both the wrong side and the
right side of each section.

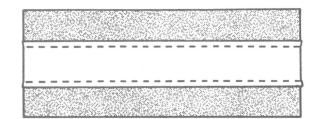

Layer the sections on the cutting mat.

Cut the sections into **3 3/4" strips** with the ruler and rotary
cutter. Use the lines on the gridded cutting mat to further
square up the sections and cut accurately.

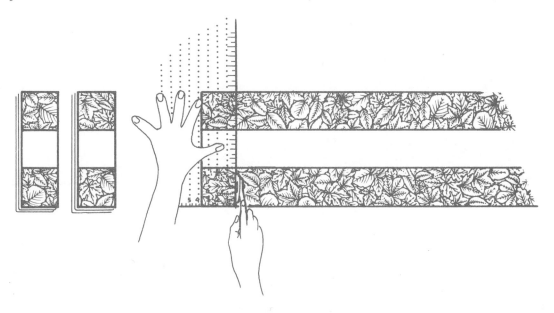

Divide the 3 3/4" strips into two equal piles.

You need this many per pile for the different sizes of quilts:

Baby	8
Lap Robe	15
Twin	20
Double	24
Queen	28
King	32

Section B (Single)

Arrange your strips in this color order.

Stack up this many strips of each color for your particular size quilt.

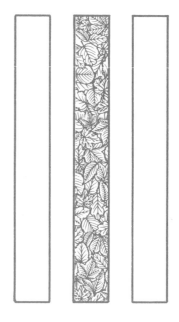

Baby	1
Lap Robe	1 1/2
Twin	2
Double	2 1/2
Queen	3
King	3

Place the dark strip right sides together to the first light strip.

1/4" seam allowance

15 stitches per inch

Stitch accurately!

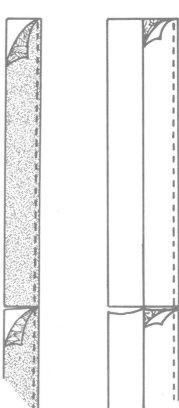

Butt on and stitch all dark and light strips.

Open up the light/dark strip.

Sew on the last light strip to all sections.

Section B (Single) looks like this:

Carefully steam press the light seams to the dark side. Press on both the wrong side and the right side of each section.

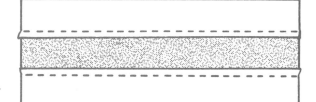

Layer the sections on the cutting mat.

Cut into **3 3/4" strips.**

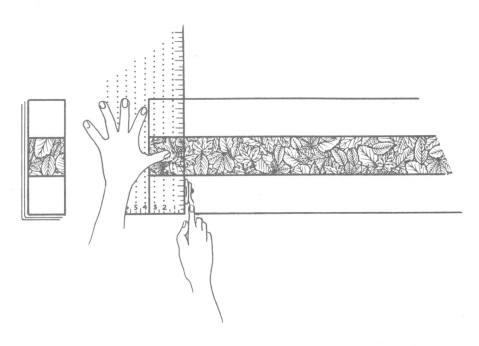

Stack the 3 3/4" strips into one pile.

You need this many for the different sizes of quilts.

Baby	8
Lap Robe	15
Twin	20
Double	24
Queen	28
King	32

Arranging the Sections to make Block 1 (Single)

With the piles, arrange them in an A, B, A order.

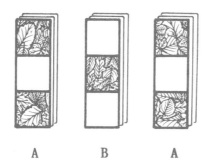

A B A

Place Section B right sides together to Section A.

Stitch down about 1/2". Stretch or ease, and fingerpin the first seam to meet. The seam allowances go in opposite directions and are easy to match.

Stitch.

Match and fingerpin the next seam.

Stitch.

Butt and stitch all Section A's and B's, matching all seams.

Open up A/B.

Assembly line sew on the last Section A .

Carefully match every seam.

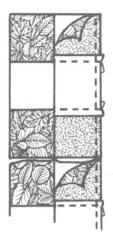

Clip the threads holding all Block 1's together.

From the wrong side, steam press the seams flat from the middle, or Section B, out.

Measure the block from one outside raw edge to the other. Measure several to find an average measurement.

Measurement:_____

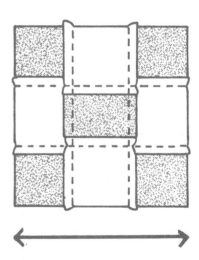

Making Block 2 (Single)

Block 2 is the exact same size as Block 1. This measurement varies between sewers, but is generally around 10" square.

Cut the light into this measurement x 45" strips.

45"

Use your own measurement!

Cut this many light strips for your particular size quilt.

Baby	2
Lap Robe	4
Twin	5
Double	6
Queen	7
King	8

Cut the light strips into the same measurement of squares.

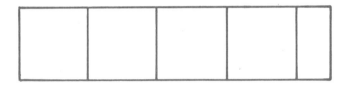

You need this many Block 2's for your particular size quilt.

Baby	8
Lap Robe	15
Twin	20
Double	24
Queen	28
King	32

Turn to page 41 for information on sewing your blocks together.

Double Irish Chain

Making the Sections for Block 1 (Double)

Completed Block 1: It is made up of Sections A, B, and C.

                    A is used twice.
                    B is used twice.
              C is used only once.

        A   B   C   B   A

Section A (Double)

Arrange your strips in this color order.

Stack up this many strips of each color for your particular size quilt.

Baby	1
Lap Robe	2
Twin Quilt	2 1/2
Double	3
Queen	3 1/2
King	4

Place a dark strip right sides together to a medium strip.

Stitch the length of the strip with a 1/4" seam allowance and 15 stitches per inch.

Be accurate with your stitching!

Use a magnetic seam guide if you have difficulty keeping a straight, accurate seam.

If you are making any larger than a baby quilt, butt on the next medium and dark strips until they are all stitched.

Add a light strip to all medium/dark strips.

Continuing in this same sewing order, add a dark strip to each section.

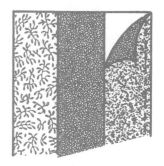

Add a medium strip to each section.

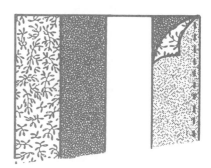

Section A looks like this:

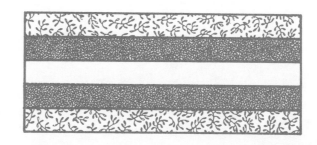

Carefully steam press all seams to one side. Press on both the wrong side and the right side of each section.

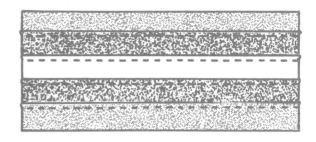

Layer the sections on the cutting mat with all seams laying away from you.

Cut the sections into 2 1/2" strips with the ruler and rotary cutter. Use the lines on the gridded cutting mat to further square up the sections and cut accurately.

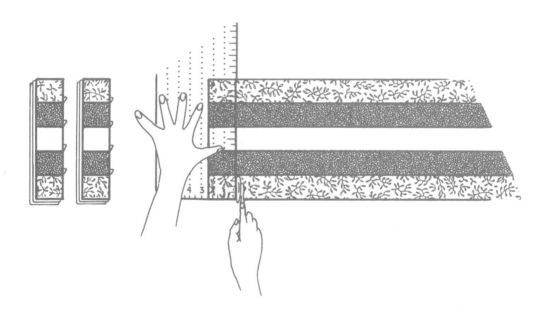

Divide the 2 1/2" strips into two equal piles as you cut. Keep the pressed seam allowances going in the same direction.

You need this many per pile for the different sizes of quilts:

Baby	8
Lap Robe	15
Twin	20
Double	24
Queen	28
King	32

Section B (Double)

Arrange your strips in this color order.

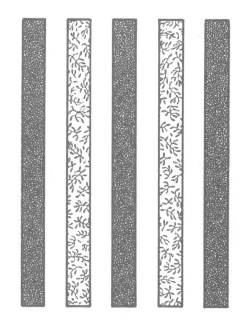

Stack up this many strips of each color for your particular size quilt.

Baby	1
Lap Robe	2
Twin Quilt	2 1/2
Double	3
Queen	3 1/2
King	4

Place a medium strip right sides together to a dark strip.

Stitch.

1/4" seam allowance

15 stitches per inch

Be accurate.

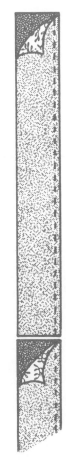

Butt on and stitch all dark and medium strips.

Add a dark strip to all dark/medium strips.

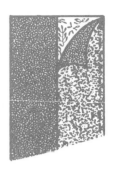

Continuing in this same sewing order, add a medium strip to each section.

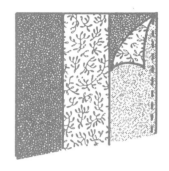

Add a dark strip to each section.

Section B looks like this:

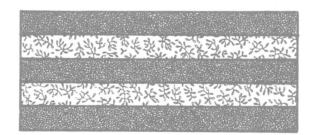

Carefully steam press all seams to one side. Press on both the wrong side and the right side of each section.

Layer the sections on the cutting mat with all seams laying away from you.

Cut the sections into 2 1/2" strips.

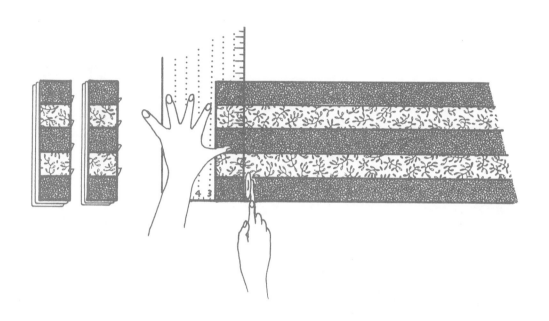

Divide the 2 1/2" strips into two equal piles as you cut. Keep the pressed seam allowances going in the same direction.

You need this many per pile for the different sizes of quilts:

Baby	8
Lap Robe	15
Twin	20
Double	24
Queen	28
King	32

Section C (Double)

Arrange your strips in this color order.

Stack up this many strips of each color for your particular size quilt.

Baby	1/2
Lap Robe	1
Twin	1 1/4
Double	1 1/2
Queen	2
King	2

Place a dark strip right sides together to a light strip.

Stitch.

1/4" seam allowance

15 stitches per inch

Be accurate!

Butt on and stitch all light and dark strips.

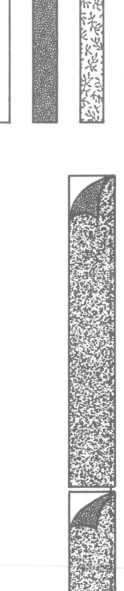

32

Add a medium strip to all light/dark strips.

Continuing in this same manner, add a dark strip to each section.

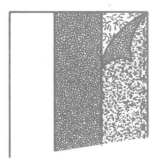

Add a light strip to each section.

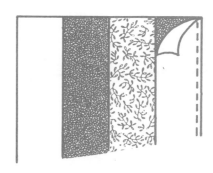

Section C looks like this:

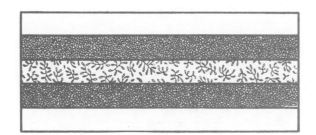

Carefully steam press all seams to one side. Press on both the wrong side and the right side of each section.

Layer the sections on the cutting mat with all seams laying away from you.

Cut the sections into 2 1/2" strips.

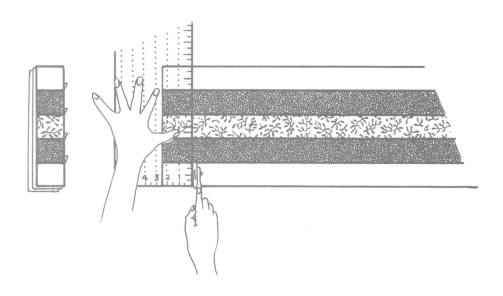

Make one pile of 2 1/2" strips. Keep the pressed seam allowance going in the same direction.

You need this many in the pile for the different sizes of quilts.

Baby	8
Lap Robe	15
Twin	20
Double	24
Queen	28
King	32

Arranging the Sections to Make Block 1 (Double)

With the piles, arrange them in an A, B, C, B, A order.

As you arrange them, turn the seams up in pile A, down in pile B, up in C, down in B, and up in A. The seams will now interlock and match easily when you sew them.

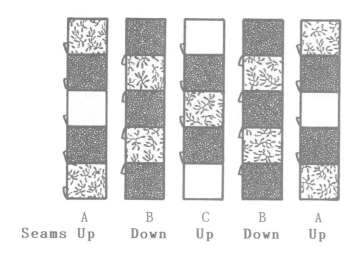

A   B   C   B   A
Seams Up   Down   Up   Down   Up

Place Section B right sides together to Section A.

Stitch down about 1/2". Stretch or ease, and fingerpin the first seams to meet. The seams will go in opposite directions.

Stitch.

Match and fingerpin the next seam.

Stitch.

Match and stitch all seams.

Butt and stitch all Section A's and B's.

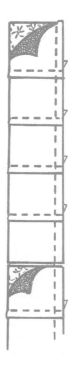

Assembly line sew on a Section C to
every Section A/B.

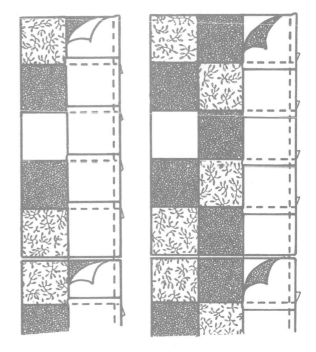

Carefully match every seam.

Add another Section B. Add the last
Section A.

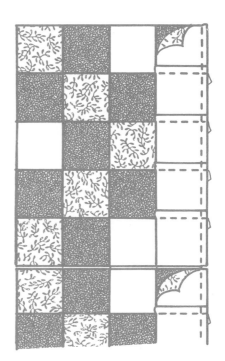

Clip the threads holding all Block
1's together.

From the wrong side, press the
seams flat from Section C out, or
the middle out on both sides.

From the wrong side, measure from
the outside raw edge of Section B
to the other outside raw edge of
Section B.

Measure several times to find an
average measurement. Include the
seam allowance.

Measurement: _____

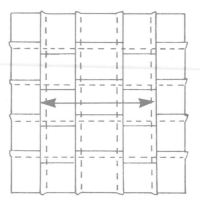

Making the Sections for Block 2 (Double)

Completed Block 2: It is made up of Sections D and E, and is the same size as Block 1.

D is used twice.
E is used only once.

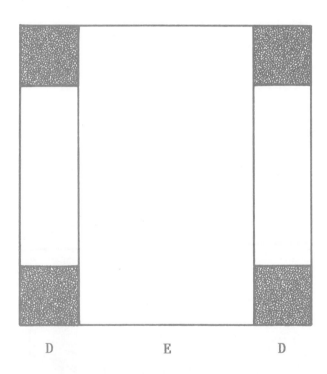

D   E   D

Section D (Double)

Use your measurement found on page 36 by measuring from the outside edge of one Section B to the other outside edge of Section B. Be certain you measured accurately so Block 2 sews together easily to Block 1. This measurement varies between sewers, but is generally 6" to 6 1/2".

Cut the light fabric into this measurement x 45" strips.

approx.
6" -
6 1/2"

45" long

Use your own measurement

Cut this many light strips for your particular size of quilt.

Baby	3
Lap Robe	6
Twin	8
Double	9
Queen	11
King	12

These are light strips for both Section D and Section E.

Arrange your strips in this color order.

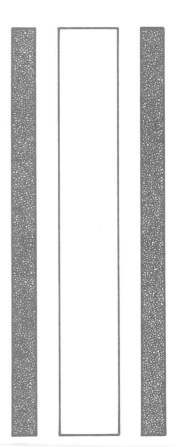

Stack up this many strips of each color for your particular size quilt.

Baby	1
Lap Robe	2
Twin	2 1/2
Double	3
Queen	3 1/2
King	4

Sew dark strips to each side of the light strips.

Carefully steam press the seams to the dark sides. Press on both the wrong side and the right side.

Cut into 2 1/2" strips.

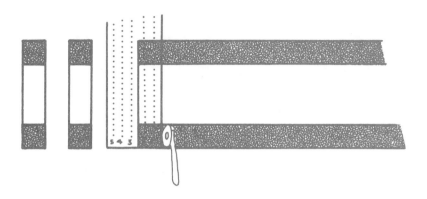

Divide the 2 1/2" strips into two equal piles as you cut.

You need this many per pile for the different sizes of quilts:

Baby	8
Lap Robe	15
Twin	20
Double	24
Queen	28
King	32

Measure Section D from outside raw edge to outside raw edge.

Measurement ────────

This measurement varies from sewer to sewer, but is generally 10" to 10 1/2" long.

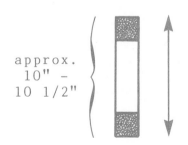

approx.
10" –
10 1/2"

Section E (Double)

Cut the remaining wide light strips into pieces the same measurement as Section D on page 39.

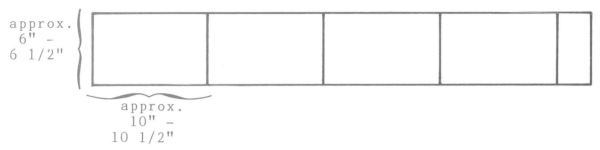

approx.
6" –
6 1/2"

approx.
10" –
10 1/2"

Use your own measurement!

You should get 4 pieces per light strip. Make this many pieces for your particular size quilt.

Baby	8
Lap Robe	15
Twin	20
Double	24
Queen	28
King	32

Arrange the piles in this order.

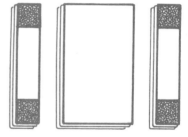

Assembly line sew a Section D onto both sides of Section E.

Clip the threads holding Block 2's together.

Press the seams flat from the middle out.

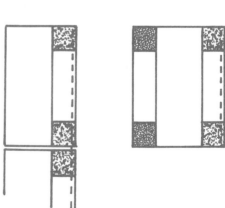

Sewing the Blocks Together

Lay out your selected size quilt following the corresponding illustration.

Alternate between Block 1 and Block 2 by beginning each row with the opposite of the block above it.

Always lay the seams in Block 2 in the same direction. (Double only.)

Baby

1	2	1	2
2	1	2	1
1	2	1	2
2	1	2	1

4 x 4

Lap

1	2	1	2	1
2	1	2	1	2
1	2	1	2	1
2	1	2	1	2
1	2	1	2	1
2	1	2	1	2

5 x 6

Twin

1	2	1	2	1
2	1	2	1	2
1	2	1	2	1
2	1	2	1	2
1	2	1	2	1
2	1	2	1	2
1	2	1	2	1
2	1	2	1	2

5 x 8

Double

1	2	1	2	1	2
2	1	2	1	2	1
1	2	1	2	1	2
2	1	2	1	2	1
1	2	1	2	1	2
2	1	2	1	2	1
1	2	1	2	1	2
2	1	2	1	2	1

6 x 8

Queen

1	2	1	2	1	2	1
2	1	2	1	2	1	2
1	2	1	2	1	2	1
2	1	2	1	2	1	2
1	2	1	2	1	2	1
2	1	2	1	2	1	2
1	2	1	2	1	2	1
2	1	2	1	2	1	2

7 x 8

King

1	2	1	2	1	2	1	2
2	1	2	1	2	1	2	1
1	2	1	2	1	2	1	2
2	1	2	1	2	1	2	1
1	2	1	2	1	2	1	2
2	1	2	1	2	1	2	1
1	2	1	2	1	2	1	2
2	1	2	1	2	1	2	1

8 x 8

Flip the second vertical row right sides together onto the first vertical row.

Pick up the pairs of blocks in the first vertical row from the bottom to the top. The pair at the top will be on the top of the stack.

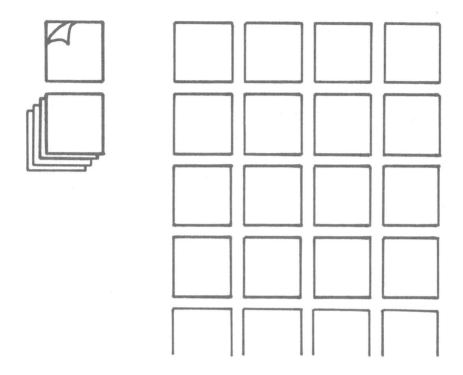

Stack up each one of the vertical rows from the bottom to the top, having the top block on the top of the stack each time.

Write the row number on a small piece of paper and pin it through all thicknesses of fabric.

Example Illustration: Your quilt may have a different number of rows.

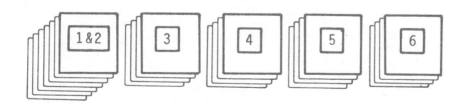

Sewing the First Two Vertical Rows

Start in the upper left hand corner. Pick up blocks #1 and #2.

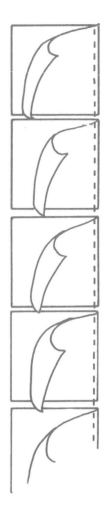

Stitch down about 1/2" to anchor the two together. Fingerpin by squeezing tightly the other corner and stretch the two to meet. Stitch.

Keep the seams turned in the same direction as they have been pressed.

Do not cut the threads or lift the presser foot.

Pick up blocks #2 and #1. Butt them right behind the first two.

Anchor the two with 1/2" of stitching. Fingerpin the corners as before. Stretch the two to meet. Stitch.

Continue butting on #1 and #2 in the same manner.

Butt and stitch all the blocks until the two rows are completed.

Do not cut the blocks apart.

Sewing the Third Vertical Row

Place Block 1 at the top of the third vertical row right sides together to #2.

Stretch and stitch the two to meet.

Butt, stretch, and stitch Block 2 in the third vertical row onto #1.

Butt, stretch, and stitch Block 1 in the third vertical row onto #2.

Continue sewing all blocks in all vertical rows in the same manner.

Do not clip the threads holding the blocks together.

Example Illustration: Yours may look different according to the size of quilt.

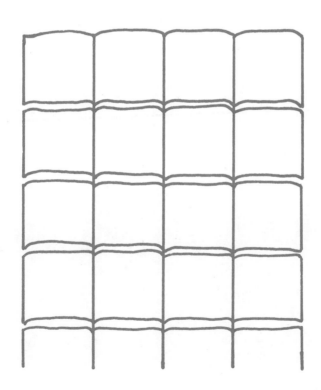

Sewing the Horizontal Rows

Flip the top row down onto the second row with right sides together.

Stretch and stitch the blocks to meet. Where the two blocks are joined by a thread, match the seam carefully. Push one seam allowance up on one side, and one down on the other side.

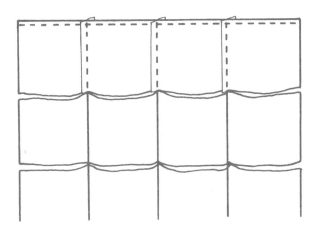

Stitch all horizontal rows in the same manner.

Sewing the Borders

Instructions for both an Easy Border and a Seminole Border are included. Refer to the Cutting or Tearing Charts on pages 8 to 13 for information on what strips to use for the borders.

Nine Patch Corners for the Borders

All nine patch corners are made with 4 1/2" strips with the exception of the 3 1/2" strips for the baby quilt with the seminole border. The baby quilt with the easy border does not have nine patch corners.

Seam two dark and one medium 37" strips together lengthwise. Press the seams flat to the dark sides. (Baby – 29")

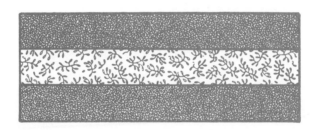

Cut into eight – 4 1/2" strips. Stack in two equal piles. (Baby – 3 1/2" strips)

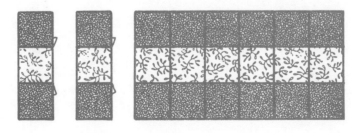

Seam two medium and one dark 19" pieces together lengthwise. Press the seams flat toward the dark side. (Baby - 15")

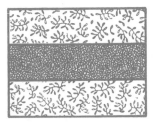

Cut into four - 4 1/2" strips. Stack in one pile. (Baby - 3 1/2" strips)

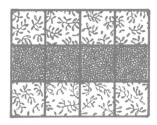

Lay the piles in this order next to your sewing machine.

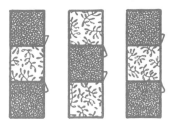

Assembly line sew all four Nine Patches together.

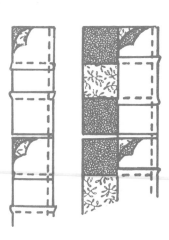

Long Border Strips

Divide the total number of medium strips in half and make two separate long medium strips.

Easy Border – Baby Quilt
Four medium strips
Do not piece together

Easy Border
Two medium strips
One dark strip

Seminole Border
Two medium strips

Seam the 4 1/2" x 45" strips into long strips by flashfeeding. (Baby - 3 1/2" x 45") Place two strips right sides together. Stitch.

Take the strip on the top and fold it so the right side is up.

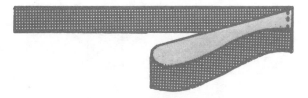

Place the third strip right sides to it. Stitch.

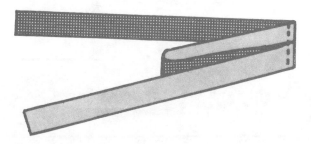

Continue flashfeeding all the short ends together into one long strip.

Clip the threads holding the long strip together.

Baby Quilt Only: Pin and sew two border pieces to two sides. Unfold. Pin and sew border pieces to the two remaining sides.

Seam the long pieces together lengthwise.

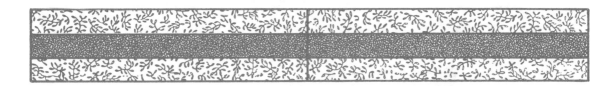

Measure the long sides of the quilt and cut two border pieces the same size.

Measure the short sides of the quilt and cut two border pieces the same size.

Pin and sew the two long border pieces to the two long sides of the quilt. Unfold.

Sew a Nine Patch onto each end of the two short border strips.

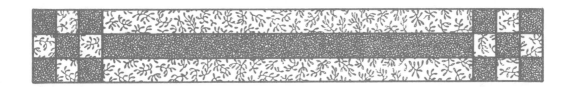

Pin and sew these strips onto each short end of the quilt.

Turn to page 55 to finish your quilt.

Seminole Border
(Optional)

This exciting addition of a seminole strip is sewn between the two medium borders. While it is not difficult, this sewing process does take time. Although the final look is dynamic, you must decide if you have time for the effort.

All seminole strips are 3 1/2" wide except for the 2 1/2" strips for the baby quilt.

Arrange your strips in this color order.

Stack up this many strips of each color for your particular size quilt.

Baby	4
Lap Robe	5
Twin	6
Double	6
Queen	6
King	7

Assembly line sew these strips together lengthwise.

1/4" seam allowance

15 stitches per inch.

Be accurate!

Press the seams to the dark side.

Layer and cut into 3 1/2" strips. (Baby – 2 1/2" strips)

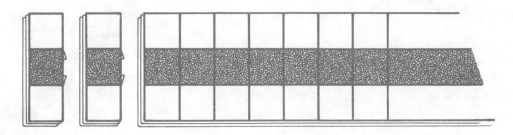

Divide them into two separate piles.

Place them so that the second piece is one step lower than the previous piece.

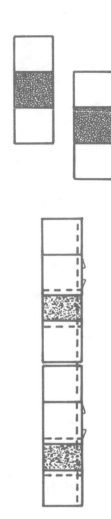

Flip the second piece right sides together to the first. The light on the top piece should extend up over the dark seam by 1/4"

Match and fingerpin the dark seam.

Stitch to the end.

Butt on, match, and stitch the second pair.

Butt on and stitch all pairs.

Clip the threads holding them together.

Stack into two piles.

Assembly line sew the pairs together, making certain that each new piece is one step lower than the previous one.

Sew all pairs into four long strips: two longer than the length of the quilt, and two longer than the width of the quilt.

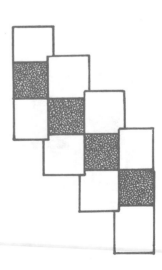

With the rotary cutter and ruler, trim off the "tips" of the seminole strip 1/4" from the seam.

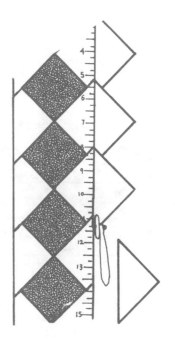

Place the seminole strip right sides together to the medium strip, with the seminole on the top.

Sew the medium strips on both sides, being careful to stitch through the "points."

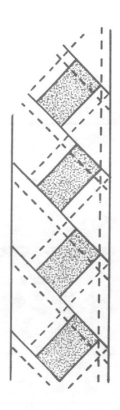

Press the seams flat toward the medium strips.

Measure the long sides of the quilt top and cut two border pieces the same size. Remember to allow the additional 1/4" seam allowance in the seminole design.

Plan carefully so that the seminole pattern is consistent on both ends. Count the number of squares in the seminole design so both sides are consistent.

Measure the short sides of the quilt top and cut two border pieces the same size. Plan the seminole design carefully.

Place the long border pieces right sides together to the quilt top.

Pin and stretch or ease the two long border pieces to the quilt top as you sew.

Sew a "nine patch" to each end of the two short border strips. The seminole block in the border has a bias stretch, and can be stretched or eased in to fit the "nine patch."

Place the two short borders right sides together to the quilt top.

Pin, ease, or stretch them as you sew.

Finishing the Quilt

Piecing the Backing Fabric

The backing may need to be pieced to get the desired length and width for the backing on the quilt.

Equally fold and cut the backing fabric into these sections:

Quilt Size	Number of Sections
Baby Quilt - Easy Border	1
Baby Quilt - Seminole Border	2
Lap Robe	2
Twin Quilt	2
Double Quilt	2
Queen Quilt	3
King Quilt	3

Seam the selvage edges of the pieces together lengthwise using the same color of thread and a 1/2" seam allowance.

If you are going to embroider your name and date on the back of your quilt, the backing fabric will now fit easily into an embroidery hoop. Consider adding your state also as many quilts end up traveling about the country.

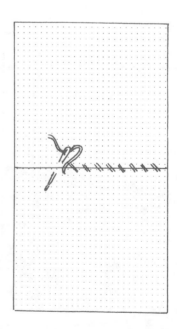

Piecing the Batting

The batting may need to be pieced to get the desired size. Cut and butt the two edges closely together without overlapping.

Whipstitch the edges together with a double strand of thread. Do not pull the threads tightly as this will create a hard ridge visible on the outside of the quilt.

Quick Turn Method

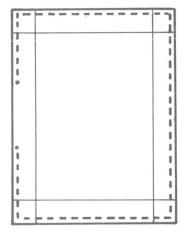

Lay the quilt top right sides together to the backing fabric. Pin.

Trim any excess backing fabric so all sides are even.

Stitch around the outside edge with a 1/4" seam allowance and 15 stitches per inch. Leave an opening in the middle of one long side approximately 24" long.

Lay the batting out on the floor or on a large table. Lay the quilt wrong side out on top of the batting. Smooth.

Cut the batting the same size as the top. **Be extremely careful** not to cut into the quilt while trimming the batting away.

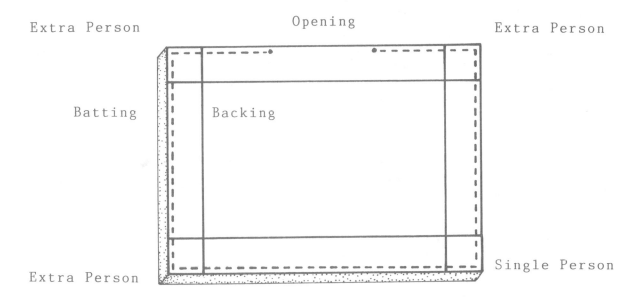

Turning the Quilt Top

This part of making your quilt is particularly exciting. One person can turn the quilt alone, but its so much fun to turn it into a 10 minute family or neighborhood event with three or four others.

Read this whole section before beginning.

If you are working with a group, station the people at the corners of the quilt. If working alone, start in one corner opposite the opening.

Roll the corners tightly to keep the batting in place. Roll the
batting along the sides as tightly as you roll toward the
opening.

If several people are helping, all
should roll toward the opening. If
only you are doing the rolling, use
your knee to hold down one corner
while stretching over to the other
corners.

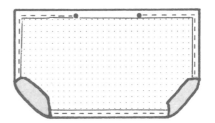

Roll all corners and sides towards
the opening.

Open up the opening over this huge
wad of fabric and batting and pop
the quilt right side out through
the hole.

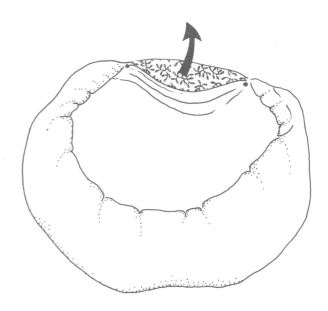

Unroll it right side out very
carefully with the layers
together.

Lay the quilt out flat.

Work out all wrinkles and bumps by stationing two people opposite
each other around the quilt. Each grasp the edge and tug the
quilt in oppposite directions.

You can also relocate any batting by reaching inside the quilt
through the opening with a yardstick. Hold the edges and shake
the batting into place if necessary.

Tying a Surgeon's Square Knot

Use a curved needle from a packaged assortment of needles. Tie with all six strands of embroidery floss, pearl cotton, wool yarn, or crochet thread.

Thread the needle with a long strand for multiple tying.

On the Single Irish Chain, tie at all the corners of Block 1 that fall in a diagonal line. Follow the diagram for the placement of the square knots on the Double Irish Chain. Tie the borders and "nine patch" corners also.

Beginning at one point, take a stitch through all thicknesses. **Do not cut the threads.**

Draw the needle over to the next point to be tied and take a stitch. **Do not cut the threads.**

Take as many continuous stitches as the length of yarn will allow, stitching through all points to be tied.

Cut all threads midway between the stitches.

Tie the yarn into a surgeon's square knot.

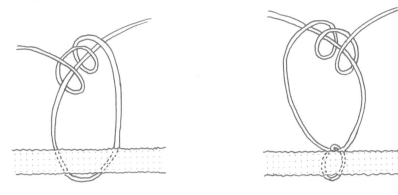

Right over left.
Wrap twice.
Pull tight.

Left over right.
Wrap twice.
Pull tight.

Clip the strands of yarn even to whatever length you wish.

Shamrock Design to Hand quilt on Block 2 (Optional)

Trace this pattern onto a piece of cardboard. Center the pattern on Block 2 and trace around it with a cloth wash-out marker or disappearing pen. Hand quilt around each shamrock.

Stitch in the Ditch (Optional)

For more dimensional borders, you may choose to "stitch in the ditch" around them rather than tie them.

Change your stitch length to 10 stitches per inch. Match your bobbin color of thread to your backing color.

You may choose to use a decorative stitch known as the serpentine stitch for "stitching in the ditch." This stitch does not need to be as accurately "in the ditch" as a straight stitch to look attractive. Quite often, this is the stitch used by manufacturers for machine quilting.

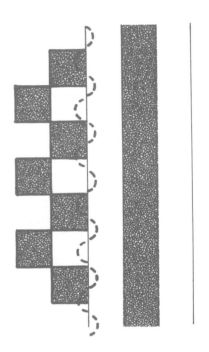

Pin along the outside edge and the inside border. Place the needle in the depth of the seam and stitch.

You can avoid puckering on the back by:

Running your hand underneath to feel for puckers,
Grasping the quilt with your left hand above the sewing machine foot,
Grasping the quilt with your right hand 10" below the sewing machine foot,
Stretching between the two as you stitch.

To further avoid puckering on the back, you may choose to use an even feed foot or walking foot available for most sewing machines.

Acknowledgements

A Special Thanks to these People

Front Cover
Kern Family - use of their beautiful Rancho Santa Fe home
Dot Dodds - pink and purple Double Irish Chain

Front Inside Cover
Belinda Guzman - purple and pink Double Irish Chain
Dee Saenz - burgundy and grey Double Irish Chain

Back Inside Cover
Cheryl Semple - blue and cream Double Irish Chain
Orion Burns - navy and white Single Irish Chain
Valerie Sullivan - green and cream Double Irish Chain

Back Cover
Eleanor Burns -brown, cream, and blue Single Irish Chain

Index

BOOK ORDER INFORMATION

If you do not have a fine quilting shop in your area, you may purchase these products from Quilt in a Day. All of Eleanor's books feature full color cover photographs and numerous detailed illustrations. Many include related pattern variations and projects.

#1001 Quilt in a Day Log Cabin

Make a beautiful Log Cabin quilt in 10-16 hours using the speed-sew techniques in this 88-page book. Concise, step-by-step directions with detailed illustrations are presented so even the beginner can find success.

#1002 The Sampler--A Machine Sewn Quilt

Complete, detailed directions and illustrations show how to speed-sew a sampler quilt. The quilt is assembled using calicos, laces and trims for a nostalgic touch. All 50 patterns are machine quilted on bonded batting for a soft, dimensional look. Instructions for smaller projects are also given. 125 pages

#1003 Trio of Treasured Quilts

Three different patterns: Monkey Wrench, Ohio Star and Bear's Paw are featured with quick, complete machine sewing methods. Make one block or a whole quilt using the convenient detailed yardage and cutting charts, as well as Eleanor Burns' assembly-line sewing techniques. This book includes projects easy enough for beginners, yet exciting enough for experienced hand quilters. 149 pages

#1004 Lover's Knot

The ease of Eleanor Burns' assembly-line sewing techniques continues in the Lover's Knot book. This traditional pattern, resembling the intertwining of two wedding bands, is quick to sew and requires only four colors. Additional features of the book include a sawtooth finished edge and a simple to sew dust ruffle. 64 pages

#1005 Amish Quilt in a Day

The versatile pattern of the "Roman Stripe" goes together easily with strip sewing and quick cutting of the blocks with a rotary cutter. Full color photographs provide examples of many pattern variations. Also described is a unique "quick-turn" method of showing the backing on the front side and mitering the corners. 46 pages

#1006 Irish Chain in a Day

Quick strip sewing and rotary cutting is all the "Luck of the Irish" you will need to put this quilt together in only a matter of hours. Perfect for a child's first quilt and beginners of all ages, the Single Irish Chain is a joy to create. Experienced sewers will enjoy the more elaborate pattern variation with the Double Irish Chain. 64 pages

#1007 Country Christmas Sewing

Sew ten festive decorations with complete full size patterns and step-by-step directions. The holiday projects include a flying angel, triangle tree, tree skirt, strip quilt stocking, and much more. 32 pages

#1008 Bunnies & Blossoms

Celebrate Spring with ten different projects ranging from the BunnySocks family, eggs, bonnets, baskets, a tooth fairy pillow, and calico roses. Some are easy enough for children to make. 32 pages

#1009 May Basket

This delightful traditional pattern has not escaped the assembly-line sewing methods of Eleanor Burns. Color it Amish in dark solids or Victorian in light calicos and lace. Even the basket handle is made easy with a quick marking, sewing and pressing technique. Instructions for pillows, shams, and wallhangings included. 64 pages

#1010 Schoolhouse Wallhanging

Easy strip piecing and assembly-line sewing come together again in the production of this traditional favorite. Absolutely no templates or complicated measuring. Complete, easy to follow directions include four layout variations: Americana Border, Star, Single Lattice, and Framed Block. 24 pages

#1011 Diamond Log Cabin Tablecloth or Treeskirt

Complete detailed illustrations will guide you through this exciting pattern quickly. Construction is based on quick assembly-line sewing and strip piecing methods from the Quilt in a Day Log Cabin book. Although the "diamonds" are made easy with rotary cutting on a 60° angle, this project is most rewarding for experienced sewers. 24 pages

#1012 Morning Star Quilt

In this beautiful traditional design for experienced sewers, an eight pointed star alternates with a chain block. Eleanor explains how to make it via all the quick piecing and assembly-line techniques that have brought her such renown among quilters. 64 pages

#1013 Trip Around the World Quilt

Discover the magic of "tubing" and then "unsewing" strips in this perfect beginner book. It is enchanting tied, or for more challenge, it is a fun machine or hand quilted project. Included are instructions on the overlock sewing machine for even quicker quilts. 56 pages

#1014 Friendship Quilt

The Friendship Quilt book commemorates Quilt in a Day's Tenth Anniversary with the Album Block featured. In addition to Eleanor's easy-to-understand strip piecing instructions, suggestions are given to help you design and assemble your own special Friendship quilt. 32 pages

#1015 Dresden Plate Quilt, a Simplified Method, by Wendy Gilbert

This book is packed with easy to understand, clearly illustrated steps for machine sewing the plates and blocks together, strip piecing a lattice and 9-patch border. 64 pages

#1016 Pineapple Quilt, a Piece of Cake, by Loretta Smith

This traditionally difficult pattern is redrafted for a contemporary look and made easier with modern tools and techniques. For the experienced quiltmaker, it is complete with choice of quilt sizes, yardage charts and easy to follow illustrations and directions. Color photographs inspire an adventure with this Pineapple. 64 pages

#1017 Radiant Star Quilt

Eleanor's book features easy strip sewing and rotary cutting on the 45° angle. Instructions for a four and six color wallhanging are included, along with a variety of quilt sizes. 64 pages

#1030 Creating With Color, by Patricia Knoechel

Written by a former art teacher, this book explains the basic concepts of combining colors in fabrics and designs. Featuring fan quilts and a fan vest, seven additional patterns are taught. 88 pages

#1047 Block Party Quilt Series One

Eleanor's original Block party quilt is made up of 12 blocks depicting an appropriate theme for each month of the year. 40 pages

#1049 Block Party Quilt Series Two

This delightful quilt is made up of 12 different blocks with a "Baskets and Flowers" theme, using Early American and country styles. 46 pages

#2001 Patchwork Santa, by LuAnn Stout

This adorable Santa measures 30" tall and can be made with a sewn or painted face. He can decorate your home during the holiday season or delight a child as a stuffed toy. Full size patterns included. 8 pages

#2002 Last Minute Gifts To Sew in a Jiffy

Nothing says "Hug Me" quite like a gift that you've made for a special friend! The nine projects in this booklet are "sew easy" children and beginners of all ages will enjoy making them. Full size patterns included. 8 pages

#2011 Dresden Plate Placemats

Combine quaint calicos and rickrack or lace for these easy country table decorations. Clear illustrations show how to speed cut and sew 16 wedges together into placemats, pillows and a tea cozy. 8 pages

#2015 Log Cabin Christmas Wreath Wallhanging

The log cabin wreath is an easy to construct, assembly-line sewn wallhanging. The pattern uses light and dark fabrics to create a wreath which becomes an impressive looking beginner's project. 16 pages

#2016 Log Cabin Christmas Tree Wallhanging

Perfect for the holidays, this wallhanging can be made in a twinkling. Utilizing assembly-line sewing methods, you will find this a delightful project to warm the Christmas spirit in your home. 16 pages

#2020 Flying Geese Quilt

Capture the beauty and symmetry of wild geese in flight. This seemingly intricate pattern is made easy thanks to Eleanor Burns' quick-sew methods. Pattern.

Call or write Quilt in a Day, 1955 Diamond Street, San Marcos, California 92069

Orders Only Call 1-800- U2 KWILT (1-800-825-9458)

For Information Call (619)591-0081